OVER IN THE ARCTIC

To Joel and Andrea
—C.S.

ISBN 0-439-40979-9

Text copyright © 2003 by Connie and Peter Roop.
Illustrations copyright © 2003 by Carol Schwartz.
All rights reserved. Published by Scholastic Inc.
SCHOLASTIC and associated logos are trademarks and/or registered trademarks of Scholastic Inc.

12 11 10 9 8 7 6 5   4 5 6 7 8/0

Printed in the U.S.A.
First printing, January 2003

Especially for Gina!

Over in the city and the country under a sky so blue
Lived a hardworking editor
And her eager writers two.

"Write!" said the editor.
"We write!" said the two.
So they wrote all day under a sky so blue.

—C.R. & P.R.

OVER IN THE ARCTIC

Connie and Peter Roop
Illustrated by Carol Schwartz

SCHOLASTIC INC.
New York Toronto London Auckland Sydney
Mexico City New Delhi Hong Kong Buenos Aires

Introduction

Over in the Arctic uses the traditional rhythms and rhymes of the folk song "Over in the Meadow," by Olive A. Wadsworth. The ocean and the land at the north pole of the earth are called the Arctic. In the winter, the Arctic is cold—the land is covered with snow and the ocean is covered with ice. In the summer, the Arctic is mild—the days are long and the nights are short. Many unusual animals and plants live in the Arctic. Terns and owls soar in the blue sky. Polar bears roam across the ice. Foxes hunt and ptarmigans hide. You can *count* on animal fun as you journey over in the Arctic.

Over in the Arctic
under the midnight sun

Lived a white polar bear
And her little cub one.
"Swim," said the mother.
"I swim," said the one.
So they swam all night under the midnight sun.

Over in the Arctic under a sky so blue
Lived a brown mother caribou
And her little calves two.
"Run," said the mother.
"We run," said the two.
So they ran all day under a sky so blue.

Over in the Arctic under the frozen sea
Lived a swift mother beluga
And her little belugas three.
"Eat," said the mother.
"We eat," said the three.
So they ate all day under the frozen sea.

Over in the Arctic along the ice-covered shore
Lived a black mother seal
And her little seals four.
"Hunt," said the mother.
"We hunt," said the four.
So they hunted all day along the ice-covered shore.

Over in the Arctic where the hungry terns dive
Lived a fat mother walrus
And her little walruses five.
"Paddle," said the mother.
"We paddle," said the five.
So they paddled all day where the hungry terns dive.

Over in the Arctic where the wildflowers mix
Lived a camouflaged ptarmigan
And her little chicks six.
"Hide," said the mother.
"We hide," said the six.
So they hid all day where the wildflowers mix.

Over in the Arctic where the tundra looks so even
Lived an arctic fox
And her little kits seven.
"Snuggle," said the mother.
"We snuggle," said the seven.
So they snuggled all night where the tundra looks so even.

Over in the Arctic where the geese migrate
Lived a snowy owl
And her little owlets eight.
"Fly," said the mother.
"We fly," said the eight.
So they flew all day where the geese migrate.

Over in the Arctic where the northern lights shine
Lived a mother wolf
And her little wolves nine.
"Howl," said the mother.
"We howl," said the nine.
So they howled all night where the northern lights shine.

Over in the Arctic where the polar bears den
Lived a herd of musk oxen,
Numbering ten.
"Circle," said the leader.
"We circle," said the ten.
So they circled all day where the polar bears den.

ARCTIC ANIMALS

arctic foxes: In the summer, arctic foxes have gray fur. Their fur turns as white as snow in the winter so they can hide better. Arctic foxes eat mice, berries, birds, and any dead animals they might find.

beluga whales: Beluga whales live in the cold Arctic water year-round. Their layers of fat, or blubber, keep them warm. Belugas are the only all-white whales.

caribou: Caribou is another name for reindeer. Caribou live in large herds. Caribou can run very fast. They migrate for many miles looking for plants to eat. Caribou have thick fur in the winter to keep them warm.

musk oxen: Musk oxen have thick fur and fat to keep them warm in the Arctic. They live in herds. Musk oxen eat grass and small plants. When a group of musk oxen are attacked by wolves, they form a circle to protect themselves.

polar bears: Polar bears live only in the Arctic. Their thick, white fur keeps them warm and hides them in the snow. Polar bears are strong swimmers. They make long journeys over the snow and ice looking for seals to eat.

ptarmigans: Ptarmigans are unusual birds. Twice a year, their feathers change color. In the winter, the feathers turn white so the ptarmigans are camouflaged in the snow. In the summer, their feathers turn brown so they can hide among the rocks and grass.

seals: Seals swim under the Arctic ice. They breathe air through holes in the ice. Seals climb onto ice and rocks to rest. Seals are very good swimmers, but they are very clumsy out of the water. Seals eat fish. Polar bears eat seals.

snowy owls: Snowy owls have white feathers in the winter and brown feathers in the summer. Snowy owls eat mice, rabbits, and other small animals. Sometimes snowy owls fly far to the south in the winter looking for food.

terns: Terns are small, swift seabirds that feed on fish. Terns have long migrations. Some Arctic terns fly all the way to Antarctica and back each year. That is more than 24,000 miles!

walruses: Walruses are big and fat. Walruses use their four strong flippers to swim very fast. Walruses have two long white tusks. They use their tusks to dig for food in the muddy ocean bottom.

wolves: Wolves are strong and fast. Wolves live in families called packs. Some packs have 20 wolves. Wolves work together as a pack to hunt caribou, musk oxen, and moose.

ARCTIC WORDS

midnight sun: In the Arctic, the sun does not set in the summer. This is because the earth is tilted more toward the sun in the summer. During the summer months, the sun shines all day and all night, even at midnight.

northern lights: The northern lights are also called the Aurora Borealis. These moving bands and streamers of bright lights sometimes glow red, green, white, purple, and orange.

tundra: Tundra means "treeless plain." Trees do not grow in the tundra because of the bitter cold and strong winds. The low, flat tundra is home to many animals and many kinds of mosses, grasses, and short bushes.

BABY ANIMAL NAMES

calves: Calves are baby caribou.

chicks: Chicks are baby ptarmigans.

cubs: Cubs are baby bears.

kits: Kits are baby foxes.

owlets: Owlets are baby owls.